" Self-Discipline Simplified "

Simplifying Discipline for Lasting Success

ROHAN MODY

Self Discipline Simplified   Micro Series

Copyright © 2024 ROHAN MODY.
All rights reserved. This book or any portion thereof may not be reproduced or used in any manner whatsoever without the express written permission of the publisher except for the use of brief quotations in a book review.
Published by Rohan Mody, in India.
First Published, September 2024.
Publisher – KINDLE DIRECT PUBLISHING

INTRODUCTION

Self-discipline doesn't have to be an endless struggle between willpower and temptation. This book will show you how to turn self-discipline into a part of your everyday life, simplifying the process so it feels manageable and achievable. You'll learn powerful strategies that are both practical and easy to apply in your life.

Whether your goals are career advancement, fitness, financial success, or personal growth, self-discipline is the key to unlocking that potential. You'll find that self-discipline isn't about punishment or rigid structure—it's about taking small, purposeful actions that lead to big results over time.

- Micro Self-Improvement Series –
Minimal Bite-sized self-improvement strategies that are easy to implement on a daily basis.

Crafted for individuals who like to
Read less, Do More!

Each book in the series focuses on one area of personal growth, offering quick, actionable tips for improvement.

TABLE OF CONTENTS :

Chapter 1: Redefining Self-Discipline 7

Chapter 2: Start With Small Wins 10

Chapter 3: Mastering Morning Routines 13

Chapter 4: Building Consistency with Habits 16

Chapter 5: Mastering Your Environment 20

Chapter 6: Overcoming Temptation and Discomfort 23

Chapter 7: Creating Discipline Through Routines............ 27

Chapter 8: Managing Your Emotions for Discipline......... 31

Chapter 9: Setting Clear Boundaries............................... 35

Chapter 10: Cultivating Long-Term Discipline 38

Final Reflection: Keeping the Momentum Alive 40

Final Thoughts: Discipline as a Journey, Not a Destination 44

Acknowledgements 45

Self Discipline Simplified   Micro Series

# Chapter 1: Redefining Self-Discipline

Self-discipline often has a negative reputation. People imagine it as a strict, joyless approach to life that involves constant self-denial. But that's far from the truth. In reality, self-discipline is about self-control and the ability to direct your actions toward your long-term goals. It's about creating habits that lead to greater freedom and enjoyment of life, not less.

When you redefine self-discipline, it stops feeling like a chore and starts becoming an empowering tool for growth. You're no longer depriving yourself; you're giving yourself more control over your time, energy, and results.

Action Step 1: Redefine Your Understanding of Discipline

- Self-reflection (10 minutes): Spend 10 minutes asking yourself what self-discipline means to you. Are you holding any negative beliefs about it? Do you see it as something that limits your freedom? By addressing these beliefs, you can start shifting your mindset.

- Reframe discipline as self-respect: Discipline is a way of respecting yourself—your goals, your time, and your future. Write down three ways in which self-discipline will help you respect yourself more (e.g., by achieving your goals, taking better care of your body, etc.).

- Example: Sarah used to think of discipline as something only for "extreme" people—athletes, CEOs, or high performers. But when she reframed self-discipline as a tool for personal freedom, she began to realize that it was the very thing missing from her life. She noticed that by staying disciplined with her morning routine, she felt more in control of her day, and as a result, was less stressed and overwhelmed.

Action Step 2: Reconnect With Your "Why"

- Clarify your goals (10 minutes): Take 10 minutes to think about why you want to develop self-discipline. What are the goals you want to achieve? Write down your top three long-term goals (e.g., starting your own business, getting in shape, becoming more financially secure).

- Link discipline to your "why": After writing down your goals, ask yourself how self-discipline will help you achieve them. For each goal, write down one specific way that discipline will get you closer to success.

For example, if your goal is to lose weight, self-discipline will help you stay consistent with workouts and meal plans, even on the days you don't feel motivated.

Chapter 2: Start With Small Wins

One of the biggest obstacles to developing self-discipline is thinking that it requires massive effort right from the start. But that's not the case. The truth is, discipline is like a muscle—it gets stronger with use. Instead of trying to make huge changes all at once, start with small, manageable tasks that give you quick wins.

Small wins build momentum. They give you the confidence to tackle bigger challenges, and over time, they create a sense of accomplishment that keeps you motivated.

Action Step 1: Set a 10-Minute Challenge

- Commit to a 10-minute task: Choose one small task that you've been putting off and commit to working on it for just 10 minutes. The key is to pick something achievable, like organizing your desk, responding to a few emails, or starting a quick workout.

- Reward yourself for completing it: After finishing the task, take a moment to acknowledge the win. Small celebrations reinforce the behavior and make it more likely you'll keep taking action.

Example Scenario:

James always struggled with staying on top of his work emails, and they piled up until it felt overwhelming. One day, he decided to try a 10-minute challenge. He set a timer and spent 10 minutes responding to as many emails as he could. Once the timer went off, he realized that he had knocked out half his inbox and felt much more in control. The small win made him feel productive, and now, he spends 10 minutes on emails every morning as part of his routine.

Action Step 2: Track Your Wins

- Habit tracker (10 minutes): Create a habit tracker that allows you to visually track your progress. It could be as simple as writing down your completed tasks in a notebook or using an app to record each small win. The visual reminder will motivate you to stay disciplined.

- Example of tracking:

Jessica, a full-time student and part-time worker, found it hard to stay disciplined with her studies. She started using a habit tracker app to mark each time she completed her daily study sessions. Over time, seeing her progress made her feel more accomplished, and she was less likely to procrastinate.

Reflection:

Small wins build confidence, and confidence leads to bigger wins. The beauty of this strategy is that it helps you feel successful early on, which is key to maintaining motivation. As you stack small wins, you'll notice that tasks that once felt difficult become easier to tackle.

Chapter 3: Mastering Morning Routines

Your morning routine is the foundation of self-discipline. It sets the tone for your entire day. If you start your day with purpose and control, you'll find it much easier to stay disciplined throughout the day. However, if your morning is chaotic or unplanned, it can feel like you're constantly playing catch-up.

The goal isn't to create a rigid, hour-long routine that overwhelms you. Instead, focus on a few key actions that ground you and give you a sense of control over your day.

Action Step 1: Create a Simple Morning Routine

- Start with 10 minutes: Your morning routine doesn't need to be complicated. Start by dedicating just 10 minutes to setting your day up for success. This could include drinking water, doing a quick meditation, stretching, or reviewing your to-do list.

- Choose 3 key activities: To avoid feeling overwhelmed, pick three activities that are most important to you in the morning. For example, your routine could be: drink water, journal for 5 minutes, and review your top tasks for the day.

Action Step 2: Plan Your Day the Night Before

- Pre-plan (10 minutes): Spend 10 minutes before bed preparing for the next day. This could include laying out your clothes, packing your bag, or reviewing your calendar. The goal is to make your morning smoother by reducing the number of decisions you need to make.

- Limit morning decisions: The fewer decisions you have to make in the morning, the more disciplined you'll feel. Pre-planning allows you to start your day with momentum and avoid decision fatigue.

Example:

Emily used to rush through her mornings, always feeling frantic and behind. By simplifying her routine to just three key actions—drinking water, reviewing her goals, and planning her day—she noticed a significant difference in how calm and focused she felt. Pre-planning her mornings the night before also helped her stay organized and disciplined with her time.

Chapter 4: Building Consistency with Habits

Self-discipline thrives on consistency. Habits are the backbone of discipline because they reduce the need for constant decision-making. When something becomes a habit, you no longer rely on sheer willpower to do it—you simply do it without thinking. Building productive habits is key to sustaining discipline in the long run.

Consistency doesn't mean perfection. It means showing up, even when you don't feel like it. The more consistent you are with small actions, the easier it becomes to stay disciplined over time.

Action Step 1: Start Small to Build Consistency

- Choose a habit you want to build: Start by identifying one habit that will have the most impact on your life. This could be something like exercising regularly, eating healthier, or working on a side project. Write it down and keep it simple.

- Commit to 10 minutes per day: To build consistency, start by committing to doing your new habit for just 10 minutes each day. The goal is to focus on showing up, not on perfection. If your goal is to exercise, commit to doing a quick workout for 10 minutes every day. If your goal is to read more, spend 10 minutes each night with a book.

- Example:

Jason wanted to start writing every day, but he found it difficult to make time for it. Instead of overwhelming himself with a big writing goal, he committed to writing for 10 minutes each morning. At first, it was just a few sentences, but over time, he built consistency, and 10 minutes often turned into 30 or more.

Action Step 2: Use Habit Stacking to Strengthen Consistency

- Pair your new habit with an existing one: To make building habits easier, use the concept of habit stacking. This means attaching your new habit to something you already do regularly. For example, if you want to start journaling every day, do it right after you brush your teeth in the morning. The existing habit acts as a trigger for the new one.

- Write down your habit stack: Choose one existing habit (something you already do daily, like drinking your morning coffee or walking your dog) and write down how you'll pair it with your new habit. For example, "After I drink my morning coffee, I will spend 10 minutes planning my day."

- Example of habit stacking:

   Rachel wanted to build a meditation practice, but struggled to remember to do it. She decided to pair her new habit with something she already did—making her morning coffee. After she finished making her coffee, she sat for 10 minutes to meditate. Over time, meditation became a natural part of her morning routine because it was tied to something she was already consistent with.

Reflection:

Building consistency doesn't require huge, sweeping changes. It's about taking small, manageable actions that you can stick with over time. When you focus on consistency, discipline becomes easier, and the results compound.

Chapter 5: Mastering Your Environment

Your environment plays a significant role in your ability to stay disciplined. If your surroundings are filled with distractions and temptations, it becomes much harder to stick to your goals. On the other hand, if you create an environment that supports your discipline, you'll find it easier to stay focused and on track.

Mastering your environment means removing distractions, setting up systems that support your goals, and creating a space where discipline comes naturally.

Action Step 1: Optimize Your Physical Environment

- Declutter your space: Spend 10 minutes decluttering your workspace or the area where you spend the most time. A clean, organized environment can help clear your mind and reduce distractions. Remove anything that doesn't serve a purpose or that causes mental clutter.

- Example of a physical environment shift:

Max found that his messy desk made it hard to focus on his work. He decided to spend 10 minutes at the end of each day organizing his desk and putting things in their proper place. Over time, this small habit helped him stay focused during work hours and reduced the stress of working in a cluttered environment.

- Set up triggers for discipline: Use visual or environmental cues to remind yourself of your goals. For example, if your goal is to exercise in the morning, lay out your workout clothes the night before so they're the first thing you see when you wake up.

Action Step 2: Manage Digital Distractions

- Limit social media and notifications: Digital distractions can be one of the biggest obstacles to self-discipline. Take 10 minutes to turn off non-essential notifications on your phone and computer. Unfollow accounts that don't add value and set limits on social media usage.

- Example of managing digital distractions:

Julia used to get distracted by social media every time she picked up her phone. She decided to take 10 minutes to reorganize her phone, moving her social media apps to a folder and turning off notifications. Now, she checks her phone less often, and when she does, she's not bombarded with distractions.

Action Step 3: Create a Focus Zone

- Designate a space for focused work: Identify one area of your home or office that will be your "focus zone." This is the place where you'll go to work on tasks that require concentration. Make sure this space is free from distractions and is set up to help you stay focused.

- Example:

Michael struggled to stay focused while working from home. He decided to create a focus zone in a corner of his living room. He removed distractions like his TV remote and set up a small desk. Over time, the act of sitting in that specific space signalled his brain that it was time to focus, making it easier to stay disciplined with his work.

Chapter 6: Overcoming Temptation and Discomfort

Self-discipline often requires resisting temptation and pushing through discomfort. Whether it's the temptation to skip a workout, eat unhealthy food, or procrastinate on a project, overcoming these urges is crucial to staying disciplined.

It's important to recognize that discomfort is temporary, but the benefits of self-discipline last much longer. By learning how to manage discomfort and resist temptation, you can stay on track with your goals.

Action Step 1: Use the 10-Minute Rule to Overcome Temptation

- Commit to 10 minutes: Whenever you're tempted to give up or skip a task, use the 10-minute rule. Commit to doing the task for just 10 minutes. This reduces the pressure and makes it easier to get started. Once you're engaged in the task, it's easier to continue beyond the 10 minutes.

-Example:

Lisa often found herself tempted to skip her evening workout, especially after a long day at work. Instead of forcing herself to commit to a full hour, she used the 10-minute rule. She told herself she only had to work out for 10 minutes. Once she started, she often found the energy to keep going, and those 10 minutes often turned into a full workout.

Action Step 2: Anticipate and Plan for Discomfort

- Prepare for challenges: Identify the areas where you typically struggle with self-discipline. Are there specific times of the day or situations when you're more likely to give in to temptation? Write these down and come up with a plan to deal with them. For example, if you tend to snack mindlessly in the afternoon, plan to have healthy snacks on hand to avoid reaching for junk food.

-Example:

David knew that he often lost focus in the afternoon and turned to junk food to stay energized. To avoid this, he planned ahead by packing healthy snacks and setting a reminder to take a quick walk when he felt his energy dip. By anticipating the challenge, he was able to stay disciplined without relying on willpower alone.

Action Step 3: Practice Mindfulness to Manage Discomfort

- Mindful awareness: When you're feeling uncomfortable or tempted to quit, take a moment to practice mindfulness. Pay attention to the physical sensations of discomfort without reacting to them. Recognize that the discomfort is temporary and will pass.

- Example of mindfulness in action:

Emma found it difficult to push through discomfort during her study sessions. She started practicing mindfulness by setting a timer for 10 minutes and focusing on her breath whenever she felt the urge to quit. Over time, this practice helped her build mental resilience and stay disciplined even during challenging tasks.

Reflection:

Overcoming temptation and discomfort is a skill that gets easier with practice. The more you push through these moments, the stronger your self-discipline becomes.

Chapter 7: Creating Discipline Through Routines

Routines are the framework that support self-discipline. When your day is structured by routines, you reduce decision fatigue, eliminate procrastination, and make it easier to follow through on your commitments. Self-discipline isn't about fighting yourself every step of the way; it's about creating a system that makes discipline almost automatic.

Routines help you conserve mental energy for the tasks that matter most. By establishing a set pattern for your mornings, evenings, and work sessions, you can cultivate self-discipline without constantly relying on willpower.

Action Step 1: Design Your Morning Routine

- Start with a 10-minute routine: A strong morning routine sets the tone for your day. Begin by creating a simple 10-minute routine that helps you focus and prepare for the day ahead. This could involve meditation, stretching, reviewing your goals, or writing down your top priorities. The key is to avoid starting your day in reactive mode (checking emails or social media) and instead focus on grounding yourself.

- Example of a morning routine:

Megan used to start her mornings by immediately checking her phone, which often left her feeling scattered. She decided to create a 10-minute routine where she spent the first few minutes journaling her goals for the day, followed by a short meditation session. This small change made a big difference in how she approached the rest of her day with clarity and discipline.

- Add structure as you progress: Once you've mastered the initial 10-minute morning routine, gradually expand it by adding more productive habits. For example, after your journaling and meditation, you could spend another 10 minutes doing a quick workout or planning your meals for the day.

Action Step 2: Build an Evening Routine for Reflection

- Wind down with purpose: Your evening routine is just as important as your morning routine. Use this time to reflect on the day, relax, and prepare for tomorrow. Take 10 minutes at the end of each day to review your accomplishments, write down what worked, and note any challenges you faced.

- Example of an evening routine:

James struggled with winding down at the end of the day and often found himself staying up late, which affected his productivity the next morning. He decided to implement a 10-minute evening routine where he reviewed his day, wrote down his priorities for the next, and spent a few minutes stretching or reading. This helped him sleep better and wake up more refreshed.

- Use reflection as a tool for discipline: During your evening routine, focus on what you did well in terms of self-discipline. Celebrate small wins and use any setbacks as learning experiences for how you can improve tomorrow.

Action Step 3: Automate Your Decision-Making with Routines

- Eliminate unnecessary decisions: Every decision you make throughout the day uses mental energy. By building routines, you eliminate the need to make certain decisions, freeing up your willpower for more important tasks. For example, if you're trying to eat healthier, plan and prep your meals at the beginning of the week so you don't have to decide what to eat every day.

- Example of automating decisions:

Sarah wanted to be more consistent with her exercise routine, but she often found herself struggling to decide when to work out. She solved this by building a routine where she exercised at the same time every morning, eliminating the need to make a daily decision. Over time, this routine became a natural part of her day.

- Batch similar tasks: Another way to streamline your day is by batching similar tasks together. For example, if you need to respond to emails or make phone calls, set aside a specific time each day to do all of them at once. This helps you stay focused and reduces mental clutter.

Reflection:

Routines create structure, and structure makes discipline easier to maintain. By designing routines that align with your goals, you'll spend less time making decisions and more time taking action.

Chapter 8: Managing Your Emotions for Discipline

Emotions play a huge role in self-discipline. When we're stressed, frustrated, or overwhelmed, it's easy to give in to distractions or bad habits. Learning how to manage your emotions is key to staying disciplined, especially when things get tough.

Discipline is not about ignoring your emotions but about understanding and working with them. By developing emotional awareness and resilience, you can maintain focus and discipline even in challenging situations.

Action Step 1: Practice Emotional Awareness

- Check in with yourself regularly: Spend 10 minutes each day checking in with your emotions. How are you feeling? What emotions are driving your actions? The more aware you are of your emotional state, the easier it becomes to manage those emotions before they affect your self-discipline.

- Example of emotional awareness:

John often found himself procrastinating when he felt overwhelmed by work. He started taking 10 minutes each morning to assess how he was feeling. If he noticed feelings of stress or anxiety, he used this time to acknowledge them and set a plan for how to manage those emotions throughout the day. This small habit helped him stay on track and avoid emotional-driven procrastination.

Action Step 2: Develop Emotional Resilience

- Build mental toughness: Discipline often requires pushing through discomfort, and building emotional resilience is key to doing so. When you face a challenging task, remind yourself that discomfort is temporary. Spend 10 minutes visualizing yourself succeeding, even in the face of adversity.

- Example of building resilience:

Emma was training for a marathon and often felt discouraged during long runs. She developed a practice of visualizing herself crossing the finish line, even when the run felt tough. This mental exercise helped her build the emotional resilience needed to keep going, both in her training and in other areas of her life.

- Use positive self-talk: When you encounter setbacks, avoid negative self-talk that can undermine your discipline. Instead, practice positive affirmations that reinforce your ability to stay disciplined. For example, instead of thinking, "I'll never get this done," tell yourself, "I'm capable of completing this task, and I will."

Action Step 3: Use Stress-Relief Techniques to Stay Focused

- Identify your stress triggers: Spend 10 minutes identifying the specific situations or tasks that trigger stress for you. Once you know your triggers, you can develop strategies to manage them before they derail your discipline. For example, if you tend to feel stressed before big presentations, develop a pre-presentation routine that helps calm your nerves.

- Example of managing stress:

   Allison often felt anxious before important meetings, which made it hard for her to stay focused and disciplined during the rest of her workday. She started practicing deep breathing exercises for 10 minutes before each meeting. This simple stress-relief technique helped her stay calm and focused, improving her overall discipline.

- Take mini breaks to reset: When emotions start to feel overwhelming, take a short break to reset. A 10-minute walk, meditation session, or even just some deep breathing can help you regain focus and stay disciplined.

Reflection:

Managing your emotions is critical to maintaining self-discipline. By developing emotional awareness and resilience, you'll be better equipped to handle challenges and stay on track with your goals.

Chapter 9: Setting Clear Boundaries

Self-discipline requires clear boundaries. Without boundaries, it's easy to get pulled in too many directions, leading to burnout and a lack of focus. Boundaries help you protect your time and energy so you can stay disciplined and prioritize what matters most.

Setting boundaries is about being intentional with your time and learning to say no to distractions, unnecessary commitments, and anything that doesn't align with your goals.

Action Step 1: Define Your Non-Negotiables

- Identify your top priorities: Spend 10 minutes listing your non-negotiables—the things that matter most to you and that you won't compromise on. These could include your health, family time, personal growth, or work goals. By defining these, you'll have a clearer sense of what you need to protect with your boundaries.

- Example of defining non-negotiables:

Chris realized that his health was suffering because he was constantly prioritizing work over exercise. He decided to make daily exercise a non-negotiable and set a boundary around his work hours to ensure he had time for it. This simple shift helped him stay disciplined in both his work and personal life.

Action Step 2: Learn to Say No

- Practice saying no with confidence: One of the biggest challenges to self-discipline is overcommitting. Practice saying no to tasks, requests, or activities that don't align with your goals. Spend 10 minutes thinking about how you can politely decline requests that don't serve your priorities.

- Example of saying no:

Lisa often found herself overwhelmed because she said yes to every social event, even when she needed time for herself. She started practicing how to say no by setting clear boundaries with her friends and colleagues, explaining that she needed to focus on her personal projects. This allowed her to stay disciplined and avoid burnout.

Action Step 3: Create Time Blocks for Focus

- Block out time for focused work: To maintain discipline, you need to create dedicated time for your most important tasks. Spend 10 minutes each day scheduling time blocks for focused work.

During these time blocks, set a boundary where you won't allow distractions, such as checking emails or answering phone calls.

- Example of time-blocking:

  Ryan struggled to stay disciplined with his writing because he was constantly interrupted by phone calls and emails. He decided to block out two hours each morning for writing, during which he turned off his phone and email notifications. This helped him stay focused and complete his writing projects on time.

Reflection:

Boundaries are the foundation of self-discipline. Without them, you'll constantly be at the mercy of distractions, other people's demands, and your own impulses. By defining your non-negotiables, practicing the art of saying no, and setting time blocks for focus, you'll protect your time and energy for what truly matters. Discipline thrives in an environment where you control your time, rather than letting outside forces dictate your schedule.

Chapter 10: Cultivating Long-Term Discipline

While short bursts of discipline can yield quick wins, true success comes from sustained discipline over the long term. Cultivating long-term discipline requires a combination of self-awareness, goal-setting, and the ability to adjust as life changes. It's not just about today's tasks; it's about building habits and systems that will carry you forward for years to come.

Self-discipline is a lifelong practice, not a one-time achievement. By focusing on long-term growth, you can turn discipline into a natural part of your daily life.

Action Step 1: Set Long-Term Goals with Short-Term Milestones

- Break big goals into smaller, manageable tasks: Long-term discipline begins with clear, actionable goals. Spend 10 minutes breaking down your long-term goals into smaller milestones that you can achieve in the short term. For example, if your goal is to write a book, your first milestone might be writing the outline, followed by completing one chapter at a time.

- Example of setting long-term goals:

Sarah had a long-term goal of launching her own business, but she often felt overwhelmed by the enormity of the task. She decided to break the goal down into smaller steps, starting with researching her market, then creating a business plan. By focusing on each small milestone, she was able to stay disciplined and make steady progress.

Action Step 2: Develop Self-Accountability

- Track your progress daily: Long-term discipline requires consistent effort, and tracking your progress is a powerful way to stay accountable. Spend 10 minutes at the end of each day reviewing what you accomplished. Celebrate your wins and note any areas where you can improve.

- Example of self-accountability:

John wanted to improve his fitness over the next year, but he struggled to stay consistent. He started tracking his workouts in a journal, noting the exercises he did and how he felt afterward. This simple practice helped him stay accountable to his long-term fitness goals and provided motivation to keep going, even on tough days.

-Sure, let's continue with a reflection on how to maintain momentum and ensure that the principles of self-discipline carry forward, even after completing the book.

Final Reflection: Keeping the Momentum Alive

By now, you've built up an impressive foundation of self-discipline. You've learned how to structure your time, maintain focus, and make choices that align with your goals. But the real challenge begins now: how do you sustain that momentum long-term? The key to long-lasting discipline lies in integrating these practices into your life, refining them as needed, and always staying open to growth.

Action Step 1: Embrace Self-Reflection as a Daily Habit

- Make reflection part of your routine: Discipline isn't static—it evolves. Take 10 minutes at the end of each day or week to reflect on your progress. What went well? Where did you falter? Use this time to course-correct and plan for the future. This small habit of reflection ensures that discipline remains a living, breathing part of your daily routine, rather than something you 'achieve' and then forget.

- Example of embracing reflection:

Emily found that her discipline started to slip after a few weeks because she wasn't checking in with herself. She implemented a nightly reflection practice, jotting down her successes and areas for improvement. This simple exercise kept her aware of her habits and allowed her to continuously refine her approach to self-discipline.

Action Step 2: Revisit Your "Why"

- Stay connected to your purpose: Discipline often fades when you lose sight of why you're pursuing your goals in the first place. Every few weeks, revisit your reasons for wanting to be disciplined. Write down why these goals matter and how they align with your values. Spending 10 minutes reconnecting with your purpose can reignite your motivation when you start to feel complacent.

- Example of reconnecting with purpose:

When Mark started to lose his motivation at work, he spent some time thinking about why he chose his career in the first place. Realizing that his work contributed to causes he deeply cared about reignited his passion, making it easier for him to maintain his self-discipline during stressful projects.

Action Step 3: Build a Support System

- Surround yourself with accountability: Self-discipline is personal, but that doesn't mean you have to go it alone. Identify people in your life who can support your journey—whether it's a mentor, a friend, or a colleague. Share your goals with them and ask for their help in holding you accountable. You might even form a discipline group where you can share progress and challenges.

- Example of building support:

Julia struggled with consistency in her exercise routine until she joined a fitness group that met three times a week. Knowing that others were counting on her to show up gave her the extra push she needed to stay disciplined, even on days when she didn't feel like working out.

Action Step 4: Celebrate Your Wins, No Matter How Small

- Acknowledge progress, even if it's incremental: Discipline isn't just about grinding away day after day. It's important to pause and celebrate your achievements, no matter how small. Taking 10 minutes to recognize what you've accomplished, whether it's sticking to a routine for a week or finishing a difficult project, can boost your morale and reinforce your commitment to discipline.

- Example of celebrating small wins:

After months of working on a major project, Liam felt overwhelmed and discouraged. But when he took a step back to reflect on how far he'd come, he realized he had made significant progress. Celebrating these small victories gave him the energy and motivation to keep going.

Action Step 5: Continue Learning and Growing

- Stay open to new methods: Discipline is not a one-size-fits-all approach. As you grow and change, so will your methods. Commit to lifelong learning and personal development. This could mean reading books on productivity, experimenting with new routines, or seeking advice from those who have mastered self-discipline. Always be willing to adapt and grow.

- Example of continuous learning:

After years of working in the same industry, Rachel noticed that her methods of maintaining discipline were becoming stale. She decided to explore new techniques by attending workshops and reading up on the latest productivity research. By staying curious and open to growth, she was able to keep her self-discipline fresh and effective.

Final Thoughts: Discipline as a Journey, Not a Destination

Self-discipline isn't a box to check off or a skill you master once and for all. It's an ongoing journey that requires continual effort, reflection, and adaptation. The key to long-term success lies in staying committed, no matter what obstacles arise, and understanding that discipline isn't about being perfect—it's about making progress.

As you continue on this journey, remember to be kind to yourself. There will be days when you falter or lose motivation, and that's okay. What matters is that you get back on track and keep moving forward. With the tools and strategies you've learned in this book, you have everything you need to simplify self-discipline and create a life of consistent growth and achievement.

Now, take that first step—what's your next disciplined action?

Acknowledgements

Self-discipline is a deeply personal journey, but no one reaches their goals alone. Thank you to everyone who has supported this process, whether by providing wisdom, accountability, or encouragement. This book is a reflection of not just the author's experiences, but the collective insights of mentors, peers, and readers who strive for self-improvement every day. To those who pick up this book and commit to the path of discipline—this is for you.

www.ingramcontent.com/pod-product-compliance
Lightning Source LLC
Chambersburg PA
CBHW030517220526
45464CB00006B/2831